THIS WALKER BOOK BELONGS TO:

_____

_____   _____

_____   _____

_____

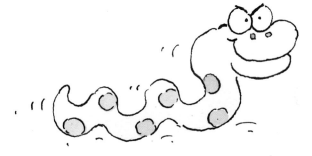

First published 1986 by Walker Books Ltd
87 Vauxhall Walk, London SE11 5HJ

This edition published 1990

Text and illustrations © 1986 Colin & Jacqui Hawkins

Printed and bound in Italy by L.E.G.O., Vicenza

British Library Cataloguing in Publication Data
Hawkins, Colin & Jacqui
Jungle sounds.
I. Title
823.'914 [J]
ISBN 0-7445-1753-2

Jungle Sounds

Colin and Jacqui Hawkins

WALKER BOOKS
LONDON

Mmm, I just love butterflies.

A panther can...

A hippo can...

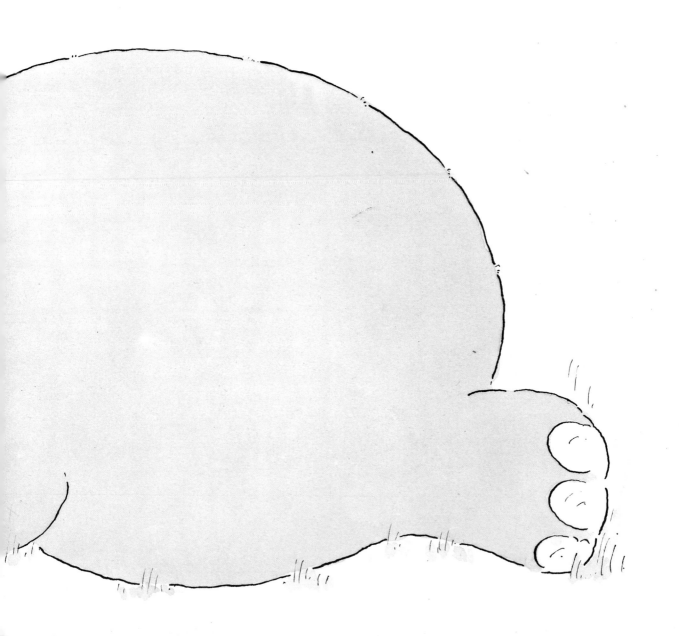

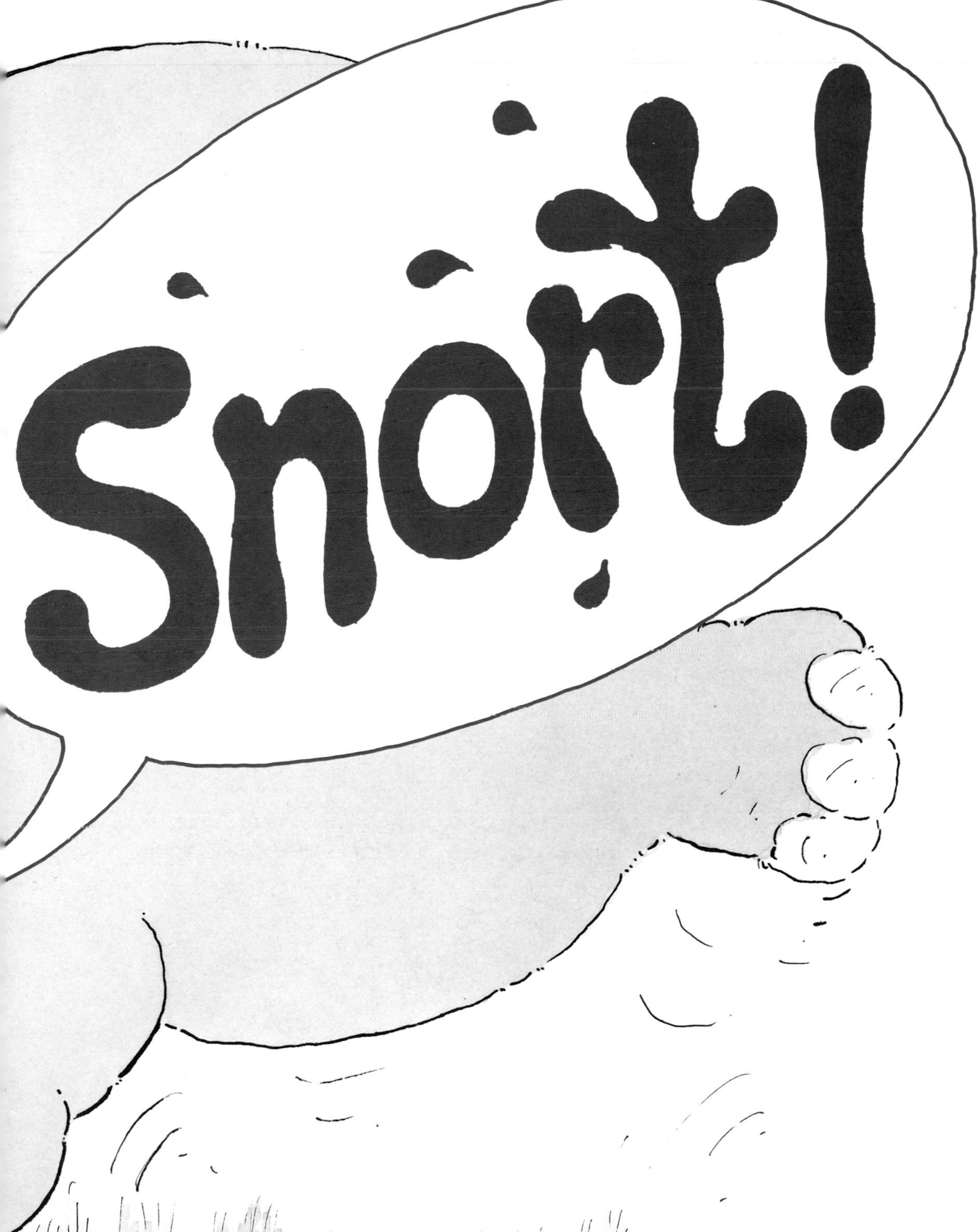
Snort!

A crocodile will…

Silly old crocodile!

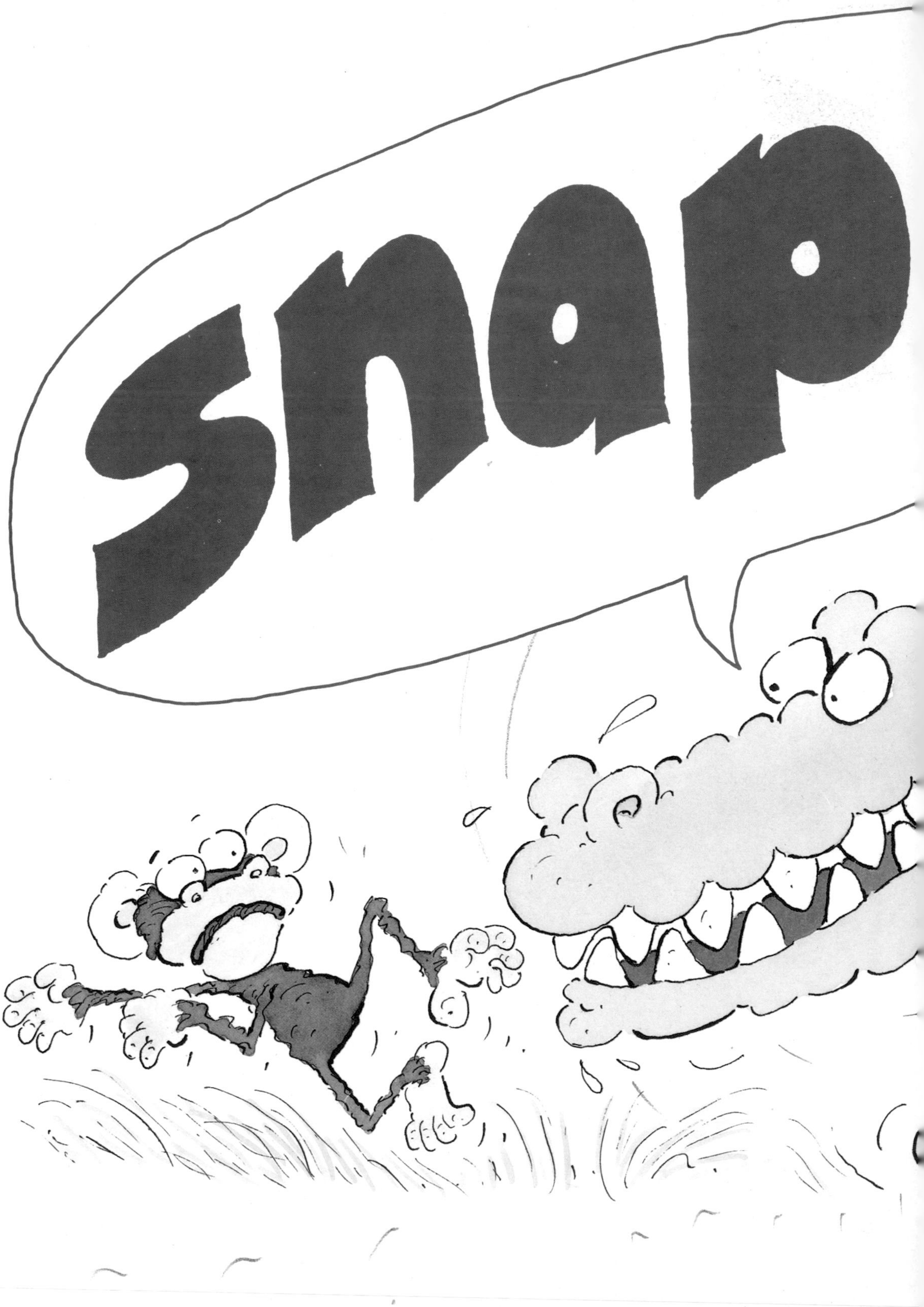
snap

Where did I put that honey?

A bear might...

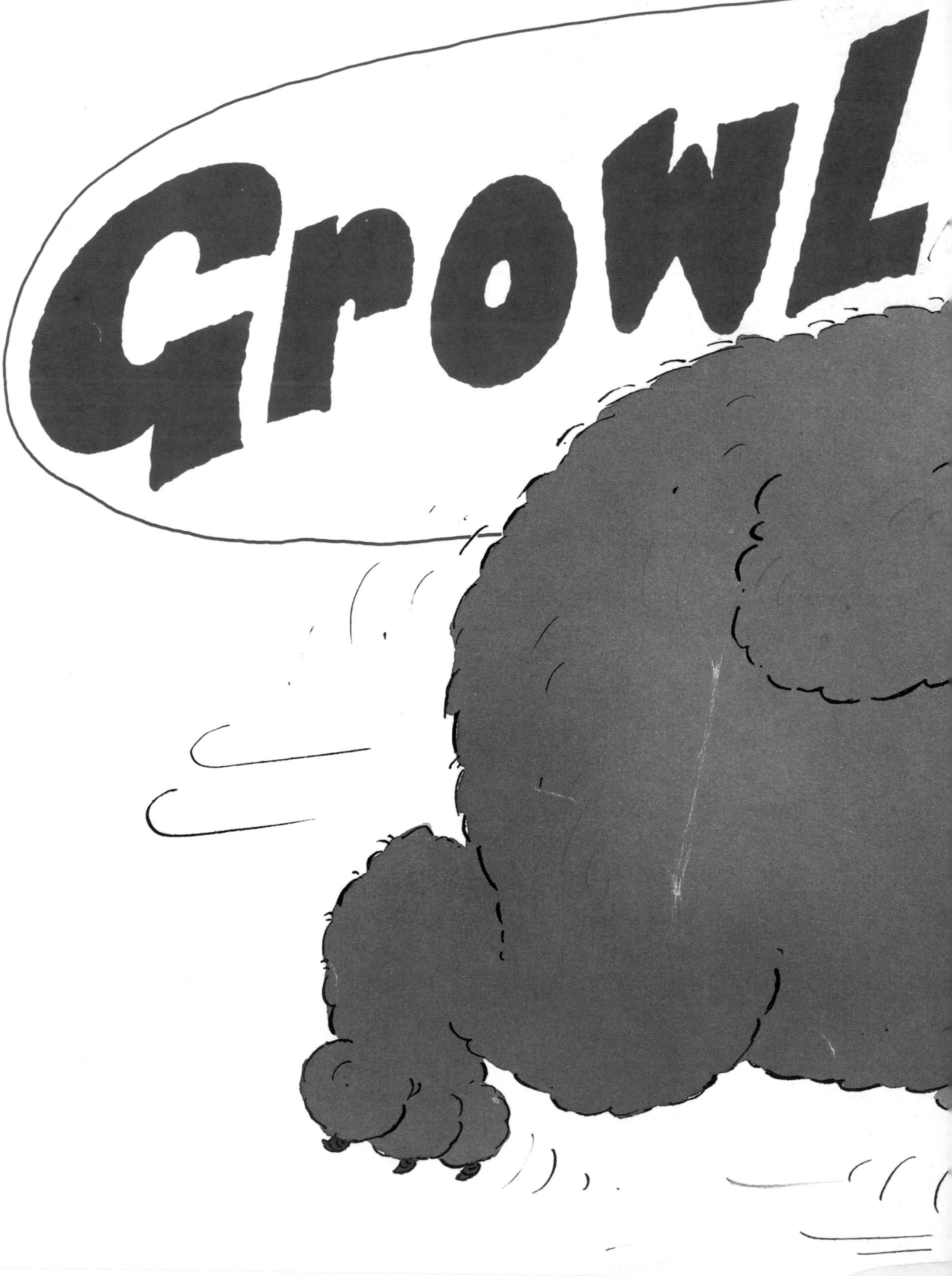
GROWL

A tiger will...

Oooh!
What a nice
fat caterpillar!

And a snake will...

Go on. Kiss him.
I dare you!

Kiss! Kiss!

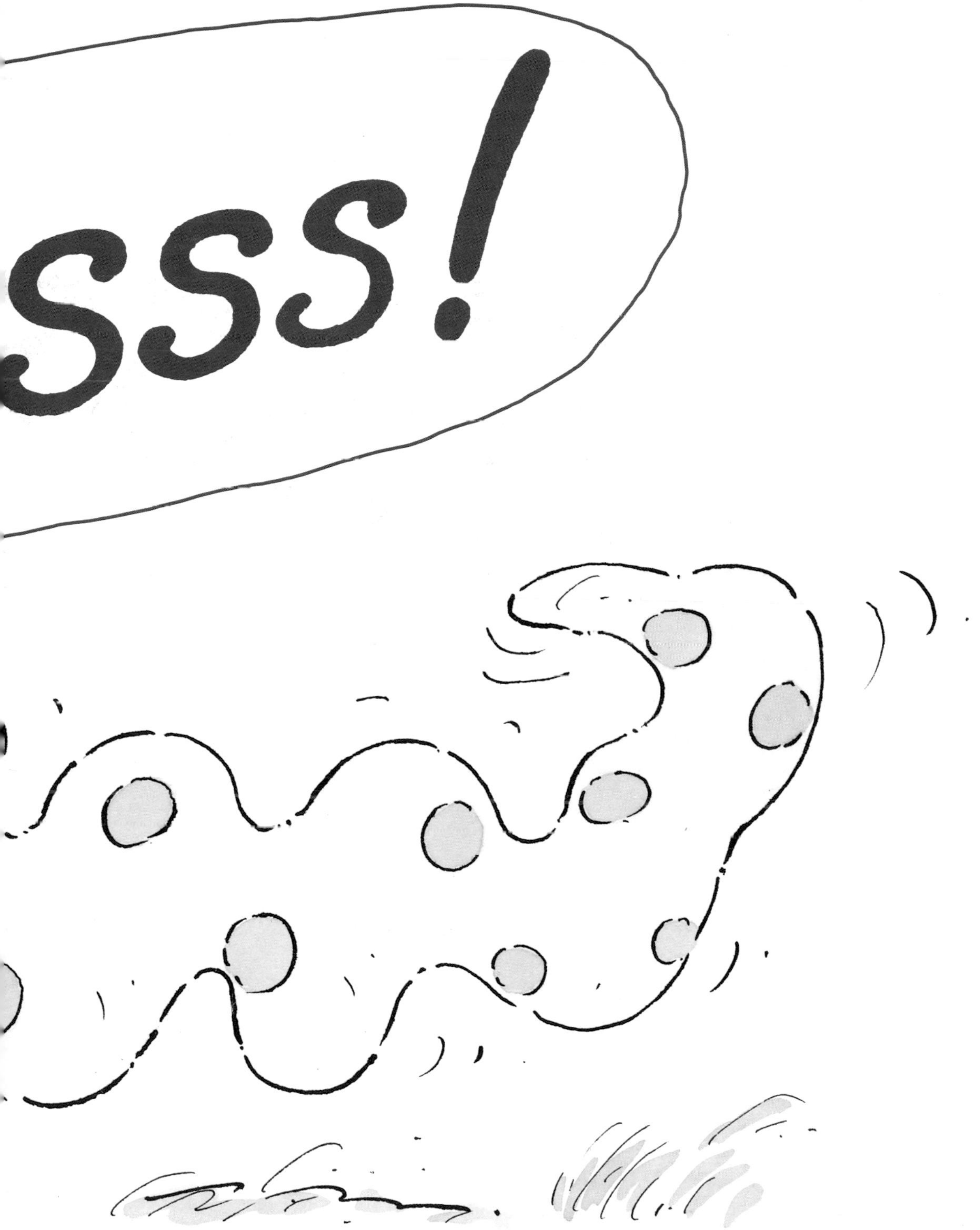
sss!

How many jungle sounds

can you make like this?

MORE WALKER PAPERBACKS
For You to Enjoy

"Quack!" said the billy-goat
by Charles Causley/Barbara Firth

Down on the farm all the animals seem to have gone quackers!
A classic rhyme illustrated by the 1988 Kate Greenaway Medallist.
"Very attractive … very funny." *Parents*
ISBN 0-7445-1442-8   £2.99

FARMYARD SOUNDS
by Colin & Jacqui Hawkins

Neigh! Baa! Quack! Moo!
How many farm sounds can you do?
ISBN 0-7445-1752-4   £2.99

TERRIBLE, TERRIBLE TIGER
THE WIZARD'S CAT
by Colin & Jacqui Hawkins

Two wonderfully entertaining rhyming picture books about a tiger who
is not quite what he seems and a cat who wishes he were something else.
Terrible, Terrible Tiger   0-7445-1063-5   £2.99
The Wizard's Cat   0-7445-1389-8   £2.99

**Walker Paperbacks are available from most booksellers, or by post from
Walker Books Ltd, PO Box 11, Falmouth, Cornwall TR10 9EN.**

To order, send:
Title, author, ISBN number and price for each book ordered
Your full name and address
Cheque or postal order for the total amount, plus postage and packing:

UK, BFPO and Eire – 50p for first book, plus 10p for
each additional book to a maximum charge of £2.00.
Overseas Customers – £1.25 for first book,
plus 25p per copy for each additional book.
Prices are correct at time of going to press, but are subject to change without notice.